SHOOTING RATS AT The BIBB COUNTY DUMP

Also by David Bottoms

Jamming With the Band at the VFW (chapbook)

SHOOTING RATS AT The BIBB COUNTY DUMP.

David Bottoms

WILLIAM MORROW AND COMPANY, INC.
New York   1980

9/1980
Eng

Library of Congress Cataloging in Publication Data

Bottoms, David.
  Shooting rats at the Bibb County Dump.

  I. Title.
PS3552.0819S5   811'.5'4   79-25724
ISBN 0-688-03609-0
ISBN 0-688-08609-8 pbk.

Printed in the United States of America

First Edition

1 2 3 4 5 6 7 8 9 10

Book Design by Michael Mauceri

for Lynn

ACKNOWLEDGMENTS

Antaeus:	"Wrestling Angels"
Atlantic Monthly:	"The Copperhead"
The Greenfield Review:	"The Orchid"
Harper's Magazine:	"The Drunk Hunter," "Shooting Rats at the Bibb County Dump"
Midwest Quarterly:	"All Systems Break Down"
Mississippi Review:	"In Jimmy's Grill"
New Letters:	"Smoking in an Open Grave"
New York Quarterly:	"Hunting on Sweetwater Creek"
Poetry:	"Crawling Out at Parties," "The Catfish," "Watching Gators at Ray Boone's Reptile Farm," "Calling Across Water at Lion Country Safari"
Prairie Schooner:	"The Sun," "The Hard Bargain"
South Carolina Review:	"Rubbing the Faces of Angels"
Southern Poetry Review:	"All Systems Tower and Collapse," "Stumptown Attends the Picture Show," "A Trucker Drives Through His Lost Youth"
The Southern Review:	"A Trucker Breaks Down," "Coasting Toward Midnight at the Southeastern Fair"
Southwest Review:	"The Traveler"
Texas Quarterly:	"After the Surgery," "The Farmers," "Speaking Into Darkness"

"Jamming With the Band at the VFW" originally appeared in *White Trash: An Anthology of Contemporary Southern Poets*, edited by Nancy Stone and Robert Waters Grey, copyright 1976 by The New South Company.

"Writing on Napkins at the Sunshine Club" and "Faith Healer Come to Rabun County" originally appeared in *Traveling America with Today's Poets,* edited by David Kherdian, copyright 1977 by the Macmillan Company.

CONTENTS

1.
INTO The DARKNESS
WE'RE HEADED FOR

The Drunk Hunter

Spun on a flat rock
his whiskey bottle points out magnetic north.
All afternoon trees stagger downhill
and up along ridges above thick brush.
He stops to watch them sway
and drinks the last of his Tennessee whiskey,
shoots the bottle off a pine stump.
Thinking there must be a logging road near
he secretly hopes that someone heard his shot,
takes time to warn he's hunting posted land.

Come morning they will praise his patience,
tell stories in camp of a tree stand
frozen over a creek, how *old Jack never would come back
empty-handed.* In two or three days
they will tell what found him in the deeper woods.

Wrestling Angels

for J. and Diana Stege

With crowbars and drag chains
we walk tonight through a valley of tombs
where the only sounds are frogs in the reeds
and the river whispering at the foot of Rose Hill
that we have come to salvage from the dead.

Only the ironwork will bring us money,
ornamental sofas overlooking graves,
black-flowered fences planted in marble,
occasionally an urn or a bronze star.

But if there is time
we shatter the hourglasses,
slaughter lambs asleep on children's graves,
break the blades off stone scythes,
the marble strings on silent lyres.
Only the angels are here to stop us, and they have grown
too weak to wrestle.
We break their arms and leave them wingless
leaning over graves like old men lamenting their age.

Shooting Rats at the Bibb County Dump

Loaded on beer and whiskey, we ride
to the dump in carloads
to turn our headlights across the wasted field,
freeze the startled eyes of rats against mounds of rubbish.

Shot in the head, they jump only once, lie still
like dead beer cans.
Shot in the gut or rump, they writhe and try to burrow
into garbage, hide in old truck tires,
rusty oil drums, cardboard boxes scattered across the mounds,
or else drag themselves on forelegs across our beams of light
toward the darkness at the edge of the dump.

It's the light they believe kills.
We drink and load again, let them crawl
for all they're worth into the darkness we're headed for.

Below Freezing on Pinelog Mountain

Crouched in the rusted cab of a junked pulpwood truck
we take shelter from freezing rain,
count bullet holes shot in the hood by hunters.

Our burden is keeping dry
while dogs follow the game into darker woods,
white breath rising from their yelps like spirits
in that song land *where the soul never dies.*
But when you pass me the bottle,
cough for the whiskey burning
cold in your throat, that same breath fogs the windshield,
rises like gray smoke through rust holes in the roof.

Scavengers at the Palm Beach County Landfill

Since a dozer buried a man from Belle Glade
even the poorest must be licensed to scavenge this landfill,
and they come in boots and red vests
fearing neither poverty nor the dozer's grave.

We back the trailer to the mouth of the pit,
dump the crippled chairs, the fractured table,
the pine frames warped around faded watercolors,
and watch the sanitation drivers resting under cabbage palms,
the dozer blades already stripping up land
to cover the tracks of the scavengers.

Like harvesters
they are moving toward us with canvas bags,
picking through our crop for aluminum and copper,
certain always that something fruitful has been discarded.

A dozer groans behind a wave of sand
and they scatter toward the edges of the pit.
Egrets fall around them like a shower of white leaves
as they wait in the palm shade,
dreaming of dumpsters,
hoping for the redemption of all things cast aside.

Smoking in an Open Grave

We bury ourselves to get high.
Huddled in this open crypt we lay the bottle, the lantern,
the papers, the bag on a marble slab,
tune the guitar to a mouth harp
and choir out the old spirituals.
When the shadows of this life have grown, I'll fly away.

Across Confederate Row an owl hoots our departure
and half-fallen brick becomes a porthole filled with stars.
We lay our ears against the clay wall;
at the foot of the hill the river whispers on its track.
It's a strange place where graves go,
so much of us already geared for the journey.

Coasting Toward Midnight at the Southeastern Fair

for Jim Seay

Stomach in my throat
I dive on rails and rise like an astronaut,
orbit this track like mercury sliding
around a crystal ball.
Below me a galaxy of green and blue neon
explodes from the midway to Industrial Boulevard,
and red taillights comet one after another
down the interstate toward Atlanta.

In the hotdog booth the Lions are sick of cotton candy.
Along the midway Hercules feels the weight of his profession,
Mother Dora sees no future
in her business,
the tattooed lady questions the reason
behind each symbol drawn indelibly beneath her flesh.

We all want to break our orbits,
float like a satellite gone wild in space,
run the risk of disintegration.
We all want to take our lives in our own hands
and hurl them out among the stars.

Cockfight in a Loxahatchee Grove

Trucks backed against the canal,
we walk with our birds toward the depth of the grove
where the moon hangs hidden in leaves
and oranges bleed shadows across black dirt.

In lantern flare
they bolt and panic in their coops, gaze hawklike
at the circle of boots and Cuban feet.
Legs spurred like thorns,
their hearts throb toward rupture like ripe fruit.
In body shelter they are brushed and calmed.

Our circle widens like the pupil of an eye,
then lanterns are hung among oranges.
Flung toward light,
the birds jerk
the leather sheaths from their spurs,
collide between us in air and blood,
caw and heat. Crippled
and dragging wings, only one crawls back into our shadow.

2.
COUNTRY AND WESTERN

A Trucker Drives Through His Lost Youth

Years ago he drove a different route.
Hauling in a stripped-out Ford
the white hill whiskey nightclubs paid good money for,
he ran backroads from Ballground to Atlanta
with the cunning of a fox,
hung on each county's dirt curves like a banking hawk.

He remembers best how driving with no headlights
the black Ford felt for the road like a bat
and how his own eyes, groping at first for moonlight,
learned to cut through darkness like an owl's.
Sometimes he drove those black roads on instinct alone.

As the shadow of a bridge falls across his face,
his rear-view says he is not the same man.
Still tonight when there is no traffic, no patrol,
no streetlight to cast shadows or light the center line,
he will search again for the spirit
behind the eyes in his rear-view mirror.
Tonight in open country in heavenly darkness
the interstate to Atlanta will crumble into gravel and sand,
median and shoulder will fall into pine forest,
and his foot will floor the stripped-out Ford
till eighteen wheels roll, roll, roll
him backwards as far as his mind will haul.

A Trucker Breaks Down

Remembering himself pulling onto a highway
in Moultrie, Georgia, is remembering a direction, firm hands,
clear eyes. All roadsigns glowed in his headlights like true
evidence of things unseen. Only now have signs begun to lie,
become no more than compasses pointing degrees
for eyes that no longer believe in north.

So he dreams of breaking down between Moultrie and
   Savannah,
his truck rolling down a backroad alone
between barbwire fences breaking into cotton fields   ⸱
breaking into forest turning into pasture
where shadows graze under moonlight falling into deeper
   darkness,
always alone moving into the solitude of all nightmares,
becoming less and less a truck hauling freight,
becoming solvent, fluid, tires melting onto blacktop
crumbling into tar and sand, separating finally into currents
of water, becoming mist downstream, becoming fog
flowing down through absolute darkness into a pool of rising
   vapor.

The Farmers

Mouth full of wet bandanna bound
to the throat with a farmer's belt,
each wrist lashed to a length of rope,
they are leading you from the green field
to the barn, to a world of animals, up steps
to strap you across the hay-strewn floor.

One ties each wrist to the base of a rafter,
another shucks the shoes, the dress,
the panties, bra, binds an ankle
to an old anvil. The rope is gone.
They are feeling over you, new mounds
of white chest, fresh hair
that gleams like gold thread fallen
into the hay. They are kissing over you,
moaning over you, speaking to each wet breast
with a different tongue.
                            You can hear the snaps,
taste the belt that once held them silent
against a farmer's belly. Hands are holding
your free leg. You close your eyes, feel
thick fingers pointing the way to the womb.
You shiver in the ropes, try to listen
to the belly-heavy mare pacing in her stall,
the cluck and scratch of hens in the yard,
anything but the thick breathing,
the life-leaving groans.
                            They swap positions.
A dog is at a cow's heels. Trucks begin
to growl in the distance. The mare is counting
time with her hoof. Crows are cawing
across the far fields. Snaps again.
                            One unties a leg,
the other a wrist. You open your eyes, struggle
with the other rope, watch them walk
down the steps, back to the fields and the reaping.

Stumptown Attends the Picture Show

on the first attempt at desegregation
in Canton, Georgia

Word has come and Martha the ticket girl
stands behind the candy counter
eating popcorn and smoking Salems.
Beside her the projectionist,
having canned Vivien Leigh
and come downstairs to watch the real show,
leans folding chairs against the theater doors,
guards his glass counter
like saloon keepers in his Westerns
guard the mirrors hung above their bars.

Outside, good old boys line the sidewalk,
string chain between parking meters
in front of the Canton Theater,
dig in like Rebs in a Kennesaw trench.
From the street policemen and sheriff's deputies
address their threats to proper names,
try to maintain any stability.
Someone has already radioed the State Boys.

Through a glass door Martha watches
the moon slide over Jones Mercantile.
In front of Landers' Drugstore
a streetlight flickers like a magic lantern,
but Martha cannot follow the plot,
neither can the projectionist.
Only one thing is certain:
elements from different worlds are converging,
spinning toward confrontation,
and the State Boys are winding down some county road,
moving in a cloud of dust toward the theater marquee.

Jamming With the Band at the VFW

I played old Country and Western
then sat alone at a table near the bandstand,
smug in the purple light
that seemed like a bruised sun
going down over Roswell, Georgia.

A short bald man in a black string tie
and a woman with a red beehive
waltzed across the floor
like something out of Lawrence Welk,
his hips moving like a metronome in baggy pants,
her following like a mirror image.

For a long time I watched and drank beer,
listened to the tear-jerking music,
thought of all my written words,
all the English classes, the workshops,
the MA stored safely under my cowboy hat,
the arty sophisticates
who attend readings in Atlanta

and weighed against them
not one bald man waltzing a woman through another Blitz,
but all men turning gray who dream of having died
at Anzio, Midway, Guadalcanal.

Then rising from my chair
I drank the last of the Pabst
and moved through the bruised light of the bandstand
onto the purple dance floor, toward the tables
across the room, toward the table beside the bar,
and there the woman with platinum hair
and rhinestone earrings, moving suddenly toward me.

Writing on Napkins at the Sunshine Club

Macon, Georgia 1970

The Rock-O-La plays Country and Western
three for a quarter and nothing recorded since 1950.
A man with a heart
tattoo had a five dollar thing for Hank and Roy,
over and over the same tunes
till someone at the bar asked to hear a woman's voice.

All night long I've been sitting in this booth
watching beehives and tight skirts,
gold earrings glowing and fading in the turning light
of a Pabst Blue Ribbon sign,
beer guts going purple and yellow and orange
around the Big Red Man pinball machine.

All night a platinum blonde has brought beer
to the table,
asked if I'm writing love letters on the folded napkins,
and I've been unable to answer her
or find any true words to set down on the wrinkled paper.
What needs to be written is caught already
in Hank's lonesome wail,
the tattooed arm of the man who's all quarters,
the hollow ring and click of the tilted Red Man,
even the low belch of the brunette behind the flippers.

In Jimmy's Grill

for Gerald Duff

The girl in bluejean shorts
walks by our table and gives us the once over,
eyes painted like we used to paint ours before ball games.
She stops at the jukebox, shifts her weight
to a stacked right heel, and the blue neon of a Budweiser sign
sparkles off the three rings in her ear.
She pushes buttons with deep red nails.

If it were only a matter of buying a few beers
or telling a lie about the money we made last year,
one of us would be asking if she has a sister.
But you only loosen your tie
and I point to the back of the room
where a beer gut rolls like a melon on the green pool table.

The Hard Bargain

In a pawnshop on Lucky Street an old Jew
sits in a wire cage, squints through thick bifocals,
and rolls a head smooth as a watch crystal
to check me in his convex mirror.

What I have brought is something from long ago.
He makes his offer and I shop
for a decision among the clutter of his shelves,
measure his degree of profit among old war medals,
watch chains, empty frames that once held pictures
of people who hocked their whole lives
piece by piece in a series of bum deals.
But there's no sense in holding out. The guitars
strung across his wall, the radios and portable TV's,
earrings and bracelets, wedding bands in his glass counter
all say he drives a hard bargain.

All Systems Tower and Collapse

for Tom Trimble

This should be a night for beer and good talk
or Tennessee whiskey and motel girls,
but tonight I drink and lie here alone
listening to walls say others have found
better company to share their darkness.
From the nightstand by the bed, Gideons
offer me the company of old words,
but their premise is all wrong. So is yours
and any philosophy that demands
the found absolute of any method.
Here's the natural gospel of it all:
all systems tower and collapse, and we
babble in darkness, seeking foundations
for other reconstructions, knowing all
along that what works always is nothing.

The Lame

Dragging the foot to the water's edge
the boy waits, watches the man in rolled shirt sleeves
raise and lower the water-logged Bible,
then steps into the red current,
dreams he feels fish gnaw the swollen ankle,
carry off in their bellies chunks of his deformity.

They meet in the middle of the river.
Kneeling at the healer's feet, water to his shoulder,
the boy listens   *a certain man lame from his mother's womb*
and at command rises, walks back across the current
fluidly toward land, toward his family's anxious eyes,
mama with her basket of fried chicken, daddy
with the family Bible, and scattered across the bank
the wondering eyes of the healed and afflicted all focused
on the river's edge, watching for the promise to emerge.

When the twisted foot breaks light, flops across sand
like a dying fish, mama closes the basket, daddy the book.
All the whole and newly healed leave the river lame.

Faith Healer Come to Rabun County

Seldom is the tent full, but tonight he expects the local radio
to draw a crowd, also the posters up for weeks
in barber shop windows, beauty parlors, convenience groceries.
Even now his boys are setting out extra folding chairs,
adjusting the P.A. for more volume, less distortion,
wheeling the piano down the ramp of a U-Haul trailer.

In the back of a red Ford van he goes over his notes
on the healing power of faith:
the woman of Canaan whose daughter was rid of a devil,
the lunatic healed who fell no longer into fires,
the Sabbath healing of the withered hand,
the spitting into the eyes of the blind man of Bethsaida
who first saw men walk as trees
and then after the laying on of hands, men as men
walking on legs among the trees.

Even now he can smell the sweat, the sawdust,
the reviving salts,
feel the healing hysteria
run electrically through charged hands,
hear the quivering lips babble into the piano music.
Who would be healed, he will say, must file to God's altar
and stand in awe at the laying on of hands,
or those unable to be in the congregation
need only lay a hand on the radio,
withered as that hand may be it will be whole.

And if all goes as he prays it will go
even the most feeble will quake down the sawdust aisle,
kneel or fall unconscious at his shocking touch
to rise strong, young, healed in the spirit.
There is medicine in the passionate heart, he will say.
There is medicine in the power of God's love

O Jesus, Savior, touch this sick brother
who accepts in faith the things we cannot know,
O sisters come to the altar, lay your hands on the radio.

3.
ALL The ANIMAL INSIDE US

Crawling Out at Parties

My old reptile loves the scotch,
the way it drugs the cells that keep him caged
in the ancient swamps of the brain.
He likes crawling out at parties
among tight-skirted girls. He takes
the gold glitter of earrings
for small yellow birds wading in shallow water,
the swish of nyloned legs for muskrats in the reeds.

But he moves awkwardly in the hardwood forests
of early American furniture, stumbles on grassy
throw rugs, and the yellow birds
flutter toward the foggy horizons of the room.
Out of date, he just can't swing
so slides back always to his antique home,
the stagnant, sobering water.

The Catfish

From a traffic jam on St. Simons bridge
I watched a fisherman break down his rod,
take bait-bucket in hand, and throw
to the pavement a catfish too small to keep.
As he walked to his car at the end of the bridge,
the fish jumped like a crippled frog, stopped
and sucked hard, straining to gill air.
Mud gathered on the belly. Sun dried the scaleless back.

I took a beach towel from the back seat
and opened the car door, walked to the curb
where the catfish swimming on the sidewalk
lay like a document on evolution.
I picked it up in the towel
and watched the quiver of its pre-crawling,
felt whiskers groping in the darkness of the alien light,
then threw it high above the concrete railing
back to the current of our breathable past.

Watching Gators at Ray Boone's Reptile Farm

While we stand behind the concrete railing
and yellow cockatoos cry through mosquito heat,
the gators never move,
but look like floating logs almost ready to sink,
wait as though long patience had taught them something
about humans,
an old voice crying up from the swamps of our brain.

Once that cry called a small boy
over the railing and the logs came alive.
A black man in a Bush hat salvaged the legs.
On the bottom of the pool
Ray Boone found a shrunken white hand clutching a stone.

Our hands clutch concrete as we lean against the railing
as though leaning might bring us closer
to that voice crying now through our common memory,
the answer to all the animal inside us.

Calling Across Water at Lion Country Safari

Across Reptile Pond a herd of zebra graze in open green
captivity, black-striped necks bent to bales of hay
dropped by natives from truck beds.
An ostrich trots into the herd
and a few colts break toward a tree by the green canal
where a giraffe neck thin as straw
needles the leaves of lower branches.

On Ape Island a gibbon moves like a gray blur
through the limbs of a leafless tree.
Below him two chimps leaning on their knuckles
watch our cars roll by in procession
something like a line of elephants in a circus.
In the back seat our Safari guide
speaks through the taped drumbeats of a darker continent,
warns against leaving cars or throwing food.

But a silverback gorilla in the mouth of a cave
sees my lens spark against the sunlight.
His hairy arm stretching slowly toward the car
curls back to his chest.
My shutter catches his eye,
the long talking arm circling in and out, calling me
across water, the only thing he believes is really between us.

Hunting On Sweetwater Creek

An old reptile at the top of my spine
knows about hunting
and leads me to this creek. And I follow blindly
through thicket and falling light, blindly
like the child I am,
a man who knows little of woods and night,
who could never find the north star.

Orange limbs darken and water turns stones sleek.
The wind says something old in the brown leaves
like those dreams
where I catch myself falling.
I sit downwind
and wait for the buck to come to water,
pause at the bank,
search for some warning the wind will not give.

Then final bearings fade
into shadow,
and the forest fills with the hissing of needles.
I listen and wait, afraid
there is something to be said for being lost
and finding again
a creature that crawls in the gut,
arcs the spine, curls hands inward toward claws,

The Copperhead

A dwarfed limb
or a fist-thick vine, he lay stretched
across a dead oak fallen into the water.
I saw him when I cast my lure
toward a cluster of stumps near the half fallen trunk,
then pulled the boat to the edge of the limbs.
One ripple ran up his back like the tail
of a wake,
and he lay still again, dark and patterned,
large on years of frogs and rats.

I worked the lure around the brush,
oak and poplar stumps rising out of the water
like the ruins of an old pier,
and watched his spade head shift on the dry bark.
But no bass struck
so I laid the rod across the floor of the boat,
sat for a long time watching the shadows
make him a part of the tree,
and wanted more than once to drift into the shaded water,
pull myself down a fallen branch toward the trunk
where he lay quiet and dangerous and unafraid,
all spine and nerve.

4.
HOW DEATH ISOLATES

All Systems Break Down

My room is quiet now. Empty, perhaps,
is a better word. I know where you are
and how the husband-hands you lie beneath
study astrologies in the small moles
of your back, trace in your constellations
systems of cosmic love. I know tonight
how death isolates the soul, erases
consciousness like darkness sucks away at
the structure of the stars. I feel how all
systems break down: how you will never sleep
without some light at the end of the hall,
how we always love in a lighted room,
how we will not trust what we cannot see,
how deeply faithless we will always be.

Learning to Let Water Heal

The coast falls away like an old skin
wedged between rocks
and we move out into the green sea.
Blue gulls follow the white boat.
Herons and gray terns,
wild horses grazing in marsh grass
scatter at our sound.
We come to Cumberland Island
to lay our bodies across the beach like broken shells.

Coming closer
Cumberland looks like an older time
darker men still belong to,
Gullahs who know the healing power of water
from dreams their fathers had of bathing wounds
in mineral-green marshes,
or Malays who drive sickness into stone animals,
or Indonesians who sprinkle the body
with water and spices,
or shamans in Borneo
who suck out sickness through bamboo tubes,
or Filipinos who pierce flesh with their hands,
reach into bodies,
remove tumors, cancers.

And how clumsy we are
at reaching behind each other's eyes
to diagnose even our most obvious need.
Somewhere on Cumberland
we must let the water turn an image back on us,
learn to look inside it and find what magic remains.

Rubbing the Faces of Angels

for Lynn

1

On the balcony of the Golden Eagle Motor Inn
a black maid pushes a linen cart.
Businessmen pass on the sidewalk below,
heels clicking like nickels on the pavement.
As she takes a key from her waist chain
and enters a darkened room,

a gray-haired man in a green turtleneck
ambles down the steps of the Gibbes Art Gallery
fighting the wind for his copy of the *Post*.
Reaching the street
he turns toward the Mills Hyatt House
where a black doorman in tophat and tails
carries luggage across a red carpet and into the lobby.

Up and down Meeting Street people are resuming routines,
but for me this is a new city and year,
a few hours to gather fresh images
while you labor across the street
in the graveyard of the Circular Congregational Church
writing in your notebook small records of the dead,
with charcoal and rice paper
rubbing the faces of angels from stones.

2

At Western Sizzler you tell me death
on the oldest stones
is a hollow-eyed skull,
sometimes over crossbones, other times wings
(later skulls grew detail,
evolved into the faces of angels),

47

and describe how the skull
cradled in bones
above the grave of David Stoddard
became the skull and wings of Desire Peronneau,
became the angel frowning over Elizabeth Mathews,
the angel rejoicing over John Gerley's grave.

After all this time, you say,
we are coming to judge death less critically.

3

The gray-haired man
is asleep in a house on some Charleston street.
Tomorrow he will walk up the same steps.
Businessmen in shiny suits will pass again
under the balcony of the Golden Eagle.
The black maid will roll her cart above their heads,
look from her balcony and watch
people from other cities, countries,
rub the same stones you rubbed today,
take photographs,
record the same sparse data of the same spent lives.
All over Charleston
things will move routinely toward one fact.

Yes, after all this time
we are coming to judge death less critically.

Even you and I
taping these rubbings
to the wall of Howard Johnson's Motor Lodge
point to this one and that
and say we'd like the figure carved on our stone,
you a smiling angel, wings curled toward heaven,
me the reclining skeleton of Thomas Pool.

5.
NO TICKET FOR The BODY TO TRAVEL ON

After the Surgery

Grandma, when I first visited
I knew your cure
wasn't written in the cards
folded over the venetian blinds.

I knew it was only a matter
of days before the roses
themselves lost their blush.

They kept you two long
months on fluids alone,
till just over half

your thriving weight
left the hospital,

a withered white bud.

The Orchid

What do you remember of me?
The last time I saw you alive you had grown
white as the hospital sheet,
a pale orchid under the oxygen tent,
strange greenhouse.

Grandma, today I saw people on television
who had been revived from death.
They told how they rose
out of their bodies and saw operating rooms,
doctors hovering above white tables.
Others saw their bodies asleep in bed
and roamed their houses as naturally
as they had in life.
Could you see me standing by your shoulder
flower like a crucifix in my hand?

Describe that face for me,
the eyes that saw the orchid bloom.

The Traveler

Where you traveled the body couldn't go,
not for the white hair washed and combed,
the cheeks flushed with rouge,
lips wired into a slight smile.
No, the body couldn't go.
In all the pockets of the new gray suit,
there was no ticket for the body.

I sat in the room of roses and carnations,
gray faces of relatives,
and watched the body stay behind
like someone seeing a traveler off on a journey,
an old man of an old world
watching his brother leave for the new.
He has lain down on a bench now
for a short rest,
no ticket for the body to travel on.

The Sun

The sun returned this morning and found you
gone, so it rose without you for the first
time in eighty-one years. I saw it climb
and watched you rest motionless on the bed
until an ambulance carted away
a statue of the man you had once been.
By early afternoon they had prepared
you for the funeral wake. Then I sensed
the same sun sliding toward my own decline.
There was no simple way to look at this.
The pale rouge face that wore the make-up mask
was proof enough of that. This was the long
crawl downhill, the long wait waiting until
the sun slides right off the edge of the world.

Nightfall brought me a change of character.
I had seen your new face a thousand times
and accustomed myself to the cold flesh.
You were becoming a science to me,
for imagination painted the rouge
on my face, turned my flesh as cold as stone,
laid me down in the steel casket beside
you, dead in the deepest hour of the night.
There I saw the similarities. You
seemed no different from the people gathered
around you. We were all the same function.
All were waiting for the same revival.
All were waiting for the sun to come up
again on the other edge of the world.

The Sun

By early afternoon they had prepared
   you for the funeral wake. Then I sensed
a statue of the man you had once been.
     the same sun sliding toward my own decline.
until an ambulance carted away
      There was no simple way to look at this.
and watched you rest motionless on the bed
       The pale rouge face that wore the make-up mask
time in eighty-one years. I saw it climb
      was proof enough of that. This was the long
gone, so it rose without you for the first
     crawl downhill, the long wait waiting until
The sun returned this morning and found you
    the sun slides right off the edge of the world.

     Nightfall brought me a change of character.
again on the other edge of the world.
    I had seen your new face a thousand times
All were waiting for the sun to come up
    and accustomed myself to the cold flesh.
All were waiting for the same revival.
    You were becoming a science to me,
around you. We were all the same function.
   for imagination painted the rouge
seemed no different than the people gathered
   on my face, turned my flesh as cold as stone,
There I saw the similarities. You
  laid me down in the steel casket beside
  you, dead in the deepest hour of the night.

Speaking Into Darkness

> *O corpse-to-be*
> Galway Kinnell

> *this night mortality wails out*
> James Dickey

1

First it was the apple
in grandma's bowel,
the way it grew to grapefruit size,
bulged beneath the hospital sheet
like a giant rotten egg,
flexed and swelled into death's pregnancy.

It was also then my mother's face
gone gaunt and pale,
her brown eyes drowning in their sockets,
grandma in the box before the fireplace,
the faces scattered around the flowered room,
their assorted expressions, gestures,
father flexing muscles in his jaw,
an uncle rubbing hands through my blond hair,
and then the knowledge in everyone's head
that somewhere in the hollows of the deep house
you sat alone in darkness behind a closed door.

2

Grandfather, later it was your own sickness,
the way it shot up your right side like high voltage,
burnt the muscles out of your arm and leg.
It was the stroke therapy,
the way mother massaged your muscles,
the small rubber ball you carried in your right hand,
the wheelchair, the cane.

It was the failure of needles, tubes, scalpels,
stethoscopes, electrocardiograms,
all things that calculate precisely
probabilities of survival.
It was all the long days you both spent dying
while medicine lost magic by degrees.
It was the loss of magic itself.

3

Faint eyes in the mirror ask the trouble.
Sometimes it's dull fireworks
exploding like oatmeal across the July sky,
men walking like frogs on the face of the moon.
Sometimes it's all the lusterless lights in Atlanta,
the foul balls carried home from Atlanta Stadium,
the splendorless ornaments
in the Sears and Roebuck Christmas Catalogue.

Sometimes these are no brighter than shadows
melting into one night,
no brighter than the grain of the door
I have closed behind me,
the room in which I sit alone tonight
studying the way my life has flexed and grown;
in the oval mirror on the wall
the texture and coloring of my beard,
the hooked, bent nose,
the muddy eyes probing
the wrinkled flesh around their lids.
Grandfather, tonight I want to be that face
moving backwards into the mirror,
want to shrink back up my mother's pink tube.

4

Eyes in the mirror say
all systems shatter like dropped glass,

collapse like the breasts of old women;
mythologies peel away like layers of an onion.

In a dream that recurs
Luke struggles in moonlight to roll away the stone.
By torchlight he unswaddles vital flesh,
examines limp joints, feels blood drifting through veins.
In his brain he rolls knowledge like dice in a cup,
administers an herbal compound.

Christ comes to Bethany in sunlight,
weeps before the tomb with Martha and Mary,
prays to God before a gallery of Jews.
In his brain he weighs
combinations of ontology and odds,
decides to gamble,
with his whole voice orders the stone be rolled away,
commands *Lazarus, come forth.*

5

And now it's this lump
stuck in my throat
like the apple Adam couldn't swallow,
the apple grandma couldn't digest.
It's the disbelief in my wife's green eyes,
the way she seldom speaks in future tense.
It's this mirror, this door, this bed,
this same darkness you closed around yourself
that time you came to this room with the New Testament
and held the book open all night in your hands.

Grandfather, I am holding no true book.
I have no orthodox dream.
My head is a kaleidoscope of crossed images:
a surgeon with a crown of thorns,
new life from the Good Shepherd Hospital.
And saying all this is pain,

like talking to your caught face hanging behind glass,
to the cedar chest, the venetian blinds,
my own eyes in the mirror.
Grandfather, I am holding nothing in my clenched hands.
Speaking into darkness is the closest I can come to prayer.

About the Author

David Bottoms was born in Canton, Georgia, in 1949. His poems have appeared in many magazines like *Atlantic Monthly, Harper's, Poetry, Antaeus, The New York Quarterly,* and others, as well as anthologies from Macmillan, William Morrow, Bantam Books, and the LSU Press. He now lives with his wife in Tallahassee where he is teaching writing courses and doing graduate work at Florida State University. An avid country music fan, he has played guitar and banjo in several Bluegrass and Country & Western bands.